Preacher, Tell Me a Story

Preacher, Tell Me a Story

HUEY WOOD

Printed in the United States of America

06   05   04   03   02   3   4   5

Library of Congress Catalog Card Number: 2001099123

ISBN: 1-57736-256-X

Cover design by Gary Bozeman

PROVIDENCE HOUSE PUBLISHERS
238 Seaboard Lane Franklin, Tennessee 37067
800-321-5692
www.providencepubcorp.com

To
my wife Ruth,
and to my children,
Mickey and Donald

Contents

Foreword

*H*ow does one communicate the most profound insights, experiences, and truths in a world dominated by fast moving images, carefully crafted sound bites, and easily erased electronic messages? How does the preacher or teacher share the timeless wisdom and enduring faith of the gospel to people unfamiliar with religious language and abstract doctrines? How can community exist without stories and collective memories that define and shape us?

Technology has increased the speed, quantity, and volume of our communication. However, few would argue that the content, quality, and depth of what is communicated have improved. The improved tools of communication have not overcome isolation and promoted community. The irony is that advanced communication tools have only intensified the need for effective means of sharing truth and creating community.

Storytelling has always been integral to communication and community. The most profound truths, poignant experiences, and penetrating insights have always been shared through stories. Stories invite others into another's experience. Stories challenge conventional thought while encouraging and honoring the dignity and integrity of the listeners. Stories bind persons together by creating a common memory and shared quest. Carefully crafted and appropriately shared stories are means of grace and transformation.

Jesus is the master storyteller. He relied on stories to communicate the profound message of the kingdom of God. They were simple stories conveying complex truth: stories of a farmer sowing seeds or harvesting crops, a homemaker looking for a lost coin, a father waiting for a returning son, a merchant in search of a precious pearl, a shepherd looking for lost sheep, fishermen casting nets, a host inviting strangers to a banquet. The stories do more than teach about the kingdom; they enable us to experience the presence and power of God.

Huey Wood knows the power of stories to transmit truth, create community, and transform lives. His life itself is a story of the gospel and how it is shared. During his many years of pastoral ministry, he has lived the story and shared it through countless stories told to diverse people. He has proven that stories bridge the gaps between rural and urban, rich and poor, old and young, black and white, the respected and the obscure. He communicates the most profound insights of the gospel to the educated and the uneducated, those sympathetic to the church and those hostile to it, those eager to hear and those distracted from hearing. At the heart of his effectiveness is his ability to tell the story through simple and often humorous stories.

This volume is more than a collection of stories that inspire, instruct, challenge, and make us laugh. The stories lead us ever so gently into the depths of the gospel and human experience. They confront us without threatening us, mold us without shattering us, challenge us without humiliating us, and transform us almost without our knowing we have been transformed. These stories and comments are means of grace!

Kenneth L. Carder
Bishop, The United Methodist Church

"A cheerful heart is a good medicine,
but a downcast spirit dries up the bones."
PROVERBS 17:22 NRSV

*T*here are many people who have trouble with Christians laughing in church. Some people have trouble with a preacher telling stories. How many times have we heard this, "I don't want a preacher to tell stories—I want him to preach the Bible." Of course when churchgoers say that, they are ignoring the fact that Jesus was the greatest storyteller of all time. He taught with parables, many of which were funny. He said, "You strain at a gnat and swallow a camel." He also said, "You are trying to get the splinter out of your neighbor's eye and you have a two-by-four in yours." Many of those who followed Jesus were following because they liked what he was saying, and because it was fun.

Someone asked Uncle Buddy Robinson one time if he believed that Jesus laughed. With that lisp in his speech he said, "Well, I don't know, but he sure fixed me to where I DO." His conversations were funny. Uncle Buddy was standing drinking a cup of coffee and a lady came up to him and said, "Preacher, do you know that it's a sin for you to drink coffee?" Uncle Buddy said, "Is that right? Who said that it was a sin for me to drink coffee?" She said, "The Lord did. He just told me to tell you that it's a sin to drink coffee, and you should stop drinking coffee." Uncle Buddy said, "Now that's strange the Lord would tell you that—you see, I've talked to him twice this morning, and He never said a thing to me about it. Are you sure you talked to the Lord?"

You see, God made us to laugh. Our physical bodies do much better when we are laughing than when we are sad and crying. Did you know that Christians are the only people on the face of this earth who have a legitimate right to laughter? The non-Christian has too many things to worry about to be laughing. A good question to ask is, What do we think Heaven will be like? I often use the word hilarious. Heaven must be a joyous, hilarious place that is filled with laughter. When I was a child, my family went to church a lot because my father was the song leader for all the revivals and baptisms, and in those days there were people who would shout. I remember that some of them would shout by laughing. What I am saying is that a good story is a parable if it is used wisely. I am thankful for stories that bring laughter.

Good storytelling has been one of the most effective methods of teaching for many, many years.

Preachers, teachers, and public speakers of all kinds have used storytelling to make their points. But good storytelling is a lost art in today's society because, rather than it being fun and something that brings laughter, it has been dragged into the gutter of filth and vulgarity. The late, great Mr. Red Skelton once said that poor language makes for poor laughter.

Storytelling is, first of all, part skill. Not everyone can tell a story effectively. There are several rules that I follow, and I think they are basic in all storytelling.

1. The story should always be to the point and not dragged out in little insignificant points. Listeners can be lost in long stories.
2. Never make a minor point a major issue.
3. Do not alter a story for personal gain. Storytelling is much more effective when credit is given to whom it belongs. Changing a story for personal gain should never happen because it makes a falsehood, which is a big no-no.
4. A good storyteller never tells a story that degrades any group, nationality, color, or gender. That, too, is a big no-no and ruins the effectiveness of anything else one might have to say.
5. Stories dealing with denominational groups can be acceptable so long as it is done in fun and love but should never be done to slander or condemn or to put down.
6. As Christians, we should never tell stories that degrade one's country, government, or elected officials. Romans 13 was written to inform us how we should think and feel toward these groups. Saint Paul is very specific, and what he said is no more out of date than anything else he had to say in this letter. Jokes and stories that degrade this land that God has given us are not funny.
7. As Christians, we should never tell a story that is not fully acceptable in mixed groups and that you would not feel free to tell if Jesus were standing here, because He *is* here.
8. A good story is designed to make people laugh. A good story comes from silly and ridiculous things we see

others doing, but we could be found doing the same silly and ridiculous things.

These are my rules, and I hope you'll enjoy reading my stories.

Acknowledgements

I would like to thank my wife Ruth, whose love, encouragement, and support has been a great part of every part of my life, and also my children Mickey and Donald and their families, who kept prodding me to compile this book. I am grateful for Bishop Kenneth Carder, whose brotherly fellowship was influential in putting these stories together. I would also like to thank Laura Cartwright who made many contacts for me; John Moore, my district superintendent and his secretary, Cheryl Denley; my local pastor and listener, Tom Buckley; David Rhea for his professional advice; Carol (Mrs. Keith) Allen for typing the final manuscript; the Treadway law firm for lending their secretary; the entire membership of my present church, Robinsonville United Methodist Church; plus those who attend and support me as great friends. Thanks are due to all members of former pastorates, Maples Memorial UMC in Olive Branch, Mississippi; Southaven First Methodist in Southaven, Mississippi; Gaines Chapel and Mt. Carmel United Methodist Churches in Corinth, Mississippi; Belmont UMC in Belmont, Mississippi; and all those churches on the Booneville circuit in Booneville, Mississippi. I thank all these members who listened to and laughed at these stories many times over and loved and supported me.

To all of you who will read and enjoy this book, I say, "Thanks!" I hope you will be blessed and smile as you read each page. May God smile on you tenderly.

Lost Watermelon

here is a story about a fellow sitting in a small restaurant trying to eat his meal. His right hand was jammed up under his armpit, and he was trying to eat with his left hand. The waitress felt sorry for him and said, "Sir, I am so sorry about your crippled arm. How did it happen?" "Crippled!" he said. "What on earth do you mean?" "Well," she replied, "with your hand up under your arm like that, I thought—" At that, he looked down, pulled his hand out, slapped his forehead, and said, "Goodness gracious, I've lost my watermelon!"

My question here is, "How in the world could a thing like this happen?" Oh, I know it's just a silly and funny story, but the point I want to make is that we often do some very foolish things that cause us to lose things more valuable than a watermelon.

For example, we can become so preoccupied with small things that we are completely unaware of greater responsibilities that we might have. We can have our eyes on small things to the point that not even a watermelon is missed because our attention is elsewhere.

You see, our purpose, and hopefully our goal, in life is to live the way God intended us to live and for the reasons He has for us to live. However, we can become so preoccupied with unimportant things that we do not realize we have missed the main goals of life until it is too late, and we have lost our watermelon.

Let me ask you: What is your watermelon? Are you absolutely sure you still have it? Check on it on a regular basis through worship.

God is Doing a Better Job Today 📖

A little boy was all dressed for Sunday school when he looked in the mirror and said to his mother, "Mother, who made me?" She said, "God made you." He saw his dad shaving, and he said, "Who made Daddy?" She said, "God made him." The boy looked at his grandfather in the den, wrinkled and gray, and the boy asked, "Who made Granddaddy?" She replied, "God made him." The boy said, "Mom, God is doing a better job today than He used to, ain't He?"

The Christian life is one of growth and improvement. In order for life to mean anything to us, we must improve, day by day. There are things that we can do that help us grow and improve. One, we grow in reading the Bible. Here we learn who we are to ourselves, to God, and to our neighbor. The Bible gives us the purpose for our being. Two, we grow and improve through prayer. In prayer we share with God our hurts, concerns, and dreams. Here we experience Him as our heavenly Father and also our friend. He always has time for us. He never laughs at our blunders. He never mocks our dreams. We are never a nuisance to Him, and we can talk to Him about anything. We grow and improve through worship with other Christians. Here we learn to share, and we learn that we do not live in the world alone. He and His church are with us.

A Little Boy and His Dog 📖

There was this story in the news a few months back about a boy and his dog. An older brother found the homeless dog and brought it home with him, but the dog took up with the younger boy and became his dog. The boy rode the school bus eight miles to school, and that mutt dog ran those eight miles to school and then back home every day. The dog followed because his master was on that bus, and he wanted to go with his master. That dog was not pure bred anything. He was just a mutt dog, but he unconditionally loved his master. The newspaper people who did this story showed the dog lying outside the school waiting in total confidence that his master would be coming out of that building at the end of the day. They also showed the dog and the boy at the close of the day, the boy in bed and the dog by his side in total contentment.

As I looked at this picture on TV and listened to the story, the more I thought that this should remind us of the greater faithfulness of our God in Jesus Christ. His love for us is true and unconditional. Every morning when we get out of bed, we can know that He loves us. In addition, at the close of the day, we can count on him to be with us.

> *Yes, He walks with me and He talks with me*
> *And He tells me I am His own*
> *And the joy we share as He tarries there*
> *None other has ever known.* [†]

This is my God, and I hope He is yours too.

[†]Words and music by C. Austin Miles, © 1989 The United Methodist Publishing House.

Holy Water 📖

A little boy was walking down the street with a bottle tied to the end of a string slinging the bottle around and around over his head. He met a Catholic priest who said to him, "Son, you should not be doing that, you might hit someone and hurt him. What do you have in that bottle anyway?" The boy answered, "It is carbolic acid." The priest said, "Why son, if you got that on someone you would hurt them. Let me trade you some of my holy water for that acid." The boy said, "Well, what will your holy water do?" The priest said, "Well, I rubbed some of it on a man's tummy up at the hospital last week, and he passed a kidney stone half the size of the end of my little finger." The boy said, "Well, that ain't nothing, I rubbed some of my stuff on my cat's tummy, and it passed a greyhound bus."

A few years after the turn of the century, engineers began moving as fast as they could to conquer speed. Now we travel faster than sound, and that's good I guess because we have come so far in this development. Nevertheless, the question we must ask of ourselves is how far have we advanced in spiritual and moral living. It's great that we can leave the east coast and get to the west coast and save time, but the question to each one of us is: What kind of people are we?

We become better people not by how fast we move, but by how we respond to the will and ways of Him who said, "I am the way." If He is the way then we may follow Him at whatever speed He is traveling. He will lead us to that good way, that higher way, that truer way, that happy and joyous way. With all of His 272 "I ams," we will arrive at the appointed time.

Cake and Pie 📖

A mother was instructing her five-year-old son in good etiquette and said if your hosts have two desserts, and they ask which you want, you should say, "I like both. I will take either one." Sure enough, the lady of the house said, "We have cake and pie, which do you want?" The little boy said, "I like either, I will take both."

This is a very cute little story, and it sounds like a five-year-old, but there is great truth in this story. It reminds us that we cannot have the whole thing. In addition, since we cannot have the whole thing, then life becomes a decision of priorities. We learn to judge if something is good or bad. So, beginning with a little thing like choosing between pie and cake, we move to the real big decisions that come when we choose between our way, someone else's way, or God's way. When we are choosing things for our lives, His way is always the right way.

The little boy in this story may have received both desserts, but two could give him a tummy ache or add unwanted extra pounds. In life we have to make choices. We cannot accept everything that is offered without considering the consequences. Mind altering substances may appear attractive for a while, but they can take control of one's life. Other habits can wreak havoc with one's health or finances. We are the ones who make the decisions. We must decide if the way we take will be our way, someone else's way, or God's way. His way is always the right way.

Eagle or Chicken 📖

here was this fellow here in north Mississippi who had a bunch of chickens and one eagle that pecked around with the chickens all the time. A local reporter heard about this and went to do a story about them. He saw the eagle and asked the farmer, "What is that eagle doing pecking around with those chickens?" The farmer said, "That's no eagle, that's a chicken." Therefore, the reporter said, "I will show you that he is an eagle. I will put him here on a high spot and show you that he's an eagle." So the reporter put him on a fence post, and he just hopped down to the ground and started pecking around like a chicken. The farmer said, "See, I told you he was a chicken." The reporter picked him up and put him on the corner of the house. Again, the eagle jumped down and started pecking around like a chicken. The farmer said, "See, I told you he was a chicken." The reporter said, "We will just go to the highest cliff we can find and throw the eagle off." This time the eagle fell for a while, but then he spread his wings and began to soar like an eagle.

Now the point of this story is that sometimes it takes someone else to see the good that is in you in order for you to accomplish and become who you were made to become. The church, with God's leadership, knows who you were made to become. In worship, God tells us that He loves us and that we can grow to be like Him. We were all made to be His very own, to be children of the King, and to represent Him on earth. At church and in the Bible, we learn what and who we are. In church, we share our strengths and weaknesses with fellow Christians.

People Make Poor Gods 📖

A lady died and arrived at the pearly gates and was very surprised to be there because she had not lived that good a life. But as she rejoiced, Saint Peter told her that she still had to pass a test in order to get in. She wanted to know what the test was and was told that she had to spell a word. It was the word *love*. She said, "L-o-v-e." "Good, you may enter," he said. She was so happy to be there that she lingered around the gate. After a while, Saint Peter asked her to watch the gate while he was away. He had not been away long when the lady's husband walked up. He too was thrilled to be there because he had not lived that well. She told him that he would have to spell a word before he could enter. "What is the word?" he asked. "The word for you," she said, "is *Czechoslovakia*."

That's a crazy story, isn't it? It's just a tall tale, but it does point out that we humans make very poor gods. We are not made to be a god. We're too weak. We're too little. We know too little. As parents, we make poor gods. As marriage partners, we make poor gods. As sweethearts, we are lousy gods. Anytime we make a human into a god, we are destined to experience heartache. No, I cannot be your god, but I can be a brother. I can be a listener, a friend, someone who cares about you. I can be a burden bearer, a prayer partner, and a helping hand. This is one reason I am a member of the Christian church. Church is where I find strength and fellowship.

Who Died?

*W*e read about two elderly fellows who met on the street, and they had not seen each other for a number of years. After visiting for a while, one of the fellows said, "Jim, I was just standing here trying to remember, was it you or your brother that died last year?" Jim replied. "Why I do not remember, you will have to ask him."

Isn't it amazing the things we can forget? As we grow older, we are capable of forgetting birthdays, anniversaries, and all kinds of dates. This is normal but is worse with some than with others. Wouldn't it be wonderful if we could be selective in the things we forget? It would be great if we could all forget a nasty attitude someone had when they were not feeling well. Or if we could forget that hasty naughty word someone spoke to us on a bad day. Or if we could forget that day when our mate was in the dumps and was not joyful or praise-giving. Wouldn't it be wonderful if we could forget the mistakes of our children? Or if we could forget that day we met a friend, but their thoughts were someplace else, and they did not speak. If we could just forget all failures of others and then remember their good. Things in worship that help us forget are hymns we sing, prayer, and God's word. Worship at church is a wonderful place to forget and remember—forget our disagreements and remember our agreements.

Grandmother's Visit 📖

A grandmother went for a visit at her daughter's home, and she and her little grandson were in the den. The little boy asked his grandmother, "Grandmother, are you going to spend the weekend?" The grandmother said, "Yes, I thought I would stay over the weekend." The grandson then said, "Well, good, then we'll get to see daddy do his new trick." The grandmother didn't fully understand and asked, "What new trick are you talking about?" The boy said, "Well, I don't know, but I heard him tell Mother last night that if you came and spent the weekend, he was gonna climb the wall, and I ain't never seen him do that before."

What we say does tend to return to us in ways that are not good. How many times have we wished we could reclaim spoken words or, better still, if we just had not spoken them? Some spoken words have a way of getting to the wrong person. If we are guilty of speaking a wrong word and, if that word gets to the wrong person, the only thing for us to do is to say to that person, "I am sorry, please forgive me."

This is why our prayer every day is so important. We know that we have need of confession, and the prayer of forgiveness should be offered to Him who knows all our sins because we know that we have missed the mark of Jesus.

As we come to Holy Communion, we come confessing and acknowledging who we are.

Rebel's Find 📖

The university's archeology department sent a group of students out in the hill country in search of artifacts. They came to an old house place where the house had fallen in; but right up around the chimney, under the pile of trash, they found a human skeleton. They pulled it out and took it back to the university lab for research. After several days, they discovered that this was the 1802 national hide-and-go-seek champion.

Another ridiculous tall tale, but isn't it amazing the things we can lose in life if we are not careful? Actually, we can lose some of our most treasured possessions. We can lose things that we would not give up for anything in the world. Oh, it would be good if we could lose some things. If we could lose some bad opinion we might have of ourselves or someone else. However, we simply must not lose some things. We must not lose our habit of Bible reading and meditation. We must not lose the habit of prayer. We must not lose the habit of saying "thanks" for any deed, large or small.

This quote I heard from E. Stanley Jones at an Ashram at Wood College.

We can lose our wealth, and it would not be our fault.
We can lose our health, and it would not be our fault.
We can lose our friends, and it would not be our fault.
We can lose our family, and it would not be our fault.
But we cannot lose our soul until we give our consent.

If that hide-and-go-seek champion was content to stay hidden until it was too late to be found, then the price was not worth it. When we worship on a regular basis, we are placing ourselves where the King of Kings sees and knows about us and knows where we are.

Arkansas Speeder

ill Mead, a friend of mine who is a retired highway patrolman from Arkansas, told me about a cop stopping this old lady for speeding. The cop said to her, "Lady, do you know that you were speeding?" Her husband was sitting on the passenger side, dirty, couldn't hear, but said, "What did he say?" "He wanted to know if we knew we were speeding," the old lady said. "Where are you going?" asked the cop. The old man asked, "and what did he say?" The old lady answered, "He wanted to know where we are going." The old lady said, "Truman." The cop said, "You know, the homeliest looking old man I have ever seen lives in Truman." The old man said, "What did he say?" The old lady responded, "Pa, he says he thinks he knows you."

Have you ever thought that there are many things, such as personal opinions of people, which we would be better off if we did not know them? What people think of us may not have one ounce of truth in it, but still we would be better off if it was kept in secret. The same is true with our opinion about others, because, you see, we can all be so wrong. Looks do not make the person. Looks are only skin deep, and when we get to the hearts of people, we may find them to be the most loving and caring people we know. Saint Paul was said to be one of those people. The same can be said about our spiritual goodness. When the pages of time are all opened, and we see what we did with the life we were given, we see the smile. Whether we were considered handsome or beautiful will not matter, but what we did with life will matter.

Desire for Choir 📖

*T*his fellow who had grown up far out on the mountainside came to the town church and liked it so much that he decided to join. He liked it so much that he wanted to become involved in everything. The man even joined the choir. However, he had a serious problem. He could not talk plain, and he had this nasal sound to his words. After two weeks the choir director came to the pastor and said, "That man is ruining my choir, pastor, you must get him out." The pastor was good at handling people and said, "Let me take care of this. I know how to take care of this problem without hurting his feelings." Therefore, he went to the gentleman and said to him, "Mr., we have decided that we need you to serve as our official greeter." The man said, with nasal sound, "Nope, I want to sing in the choir." A week later the preacher came back and said, "We have decided that the church needs you to be in charge of the money, to be our official counter." Again, the man said, "Nope, I am doing what I want to do. I want to sing in the choir." The preacher said, "Well, I'll just have to tell you, they say that you cannot sing." The man said, "Is that right? How many people have you heard say that?" The preacher said, "Well, three or four have said it." The man said, "Well, that ain't nothing. I have heard a dozen say you can't preach."

It is said that the most difficult part of the human body to control is the tongue. The tongue flings out cruel words, thoughtless words, and wicked words. Words that crush friendships, divide families, destroy love, and start wars. In addition, at the same time, the tongue is God's greatest gift to us. The tongue speaks words of love. The tongue speaks the words of a great hymn or love song. The tongue carries the words of the Bible, giving us hope.

Scary Kiss 📖

This old bachelor had a date with this unclaimed jewel, an old maid, back in the horse and buggy days. They were riding down the road, and neither one was saying anything. They came to this lonely place in the road, and the old fellow just leaned over and planted a big kiss on her cheek. She jumped and said, "You scared me." Nothing else was said for a while, and then they came to another lonely place in the road, and she said softly, "You can scare me again if you want to."

Often when I think of this story, I think of it in the realm of religion. I think of all that we miss out on because of our spiritual timidity. We do not even ask God for the finer things of life. When we talk to Him, we hesitate to share with Him our innermost desires. You see, we clearly forget that He is concerned about all our desires. One of my favorite songs has these words: "His eye is on the sparrow, and I know He is watching me." Yes, *me*. If He is watching me, there has to be a purpose. If He knows the number of hairs on my head, then He knows about all my feelings and my desires. As the assembled church, He is always in our midst.

Airplane Ride

L ong ago, in the early days of flight, small one-engine planes would land in hayfields at the edge of small towns, and they would take passengers up for five dollars each. On this one particular day, everyone had gone up but this one old couple. The pilot went over to them and said, "Let me make a deal with you. I will take you both up for the price of one." The old man said, "We can live a long time off five dollars." "Well," said the pilot, "let me tell you what. I'll take you both up, and if you say anything you will owe me five dollars, but if you don't say anything, the ride is free." They agreed and put the old lady in the backseat and the old man up beside the pilot. The pilot strapped them in and took off. Once they were airborne, the pilot did loop the loops, high dives, and rollovers, but the old man just sat there, griping his five-dollar bill. Finally, the pilot landed the plane and said to the old man, "Sir, I was sure I could make you talk, but you never said a word." The old man looked at him and said, "Nope, but I thought I was gonna when the old woman fell out."

Miserliness is in the air we breathe. Some people are miserly with their talent or with their wealth. Others are miserly with their time. We all have the same amount of time, but we can allow ourselves to become so busy that we do not have time for family and the finer things of life. Lack of time is a problem for all of us in that we put so many things that have nothing to do with our eternal life first in our time.

Happy Birthday 📖

A fellow was on his way home from work, and he just happened to remember that it was his wife's birthday. He went to a candy store and got her a box of chocolates, and then he stopped by the flower shop and bought her one dozen red roses. When he got home he found her in the kitchen and grabbed her and kissed her and said, "HAPPY BIRTHDAY, I LOVE YOU." She began to cry and said, "This is the worst day of my life. The washing machine broke, the dishwasher stopped up, the kids have cried all day, and now you've come home drunk."

One of the things about being good and doing good deeds is that they should be a common practice. It's not that we should give candy and flowers everyday, but we always ought to have a giving attitude so our loved ones are not surprised as the wife was in this story. This is one of the marks of the Christian listed by Saint Paul when he wrote, "And the fruit of the spirit is love, joy, peace, patience, kindness, goodness, faithfulness, gentleness, and self-control. These are gifts of the Spirit, ours for the taking, and we are not whole without them all. They cannot be turned on or off by the one who has them" (Gal. 5:22–23a KJV). Coming to church does not make one good, but it helps to be with those who are traveling in the same direction.

Arkansas Flood 📖

nce there was a huge flood in Arkansas leaving two little boys sitting up on top of a house waiting to be rescued by a helicopter. Out in front of the house they saw a straw hat going back and forth across the yard. At first they couldn't figure out what was causing it to do this until one of them said, "Oh, I know what that is. That's Grandpa! I heard him say day before yesterday that he was going to mow this yard today come hail or high water."

Determination is a wonderful thing, isn't it? Especially if it's for a good cause. In thinking about the power of determination we ask: What if every member of any church would say, "Come hail or high water, I will be present when the congregation is meeting"? And what if I determine to bring my tithe; what if I determine to pray for my church; what if I determine to visit the unchurched persons in my community?

No, I can't say whether this man was mowing, but I do know some persons who are determined to attend, to pray, and to give. This determination brings peace and joy.

Family Tree 📖

There once was a lady who decided that she wanted to do her family tree. Everyone she knew about in the family had been outstanding citizens and great people. She wanted everyone to know about her great heritage, so she set out to find all her family members. She had done quite well until she came to Uncle Josh. She had not known about him and soon wished she had never found out about him. He spent most of his life in the penitentiary and wound up being executed in the electric chair. At first, she didn't know what to do about him, but then she decided to list him like this:

"Uncle Josh occupied the chair of applied electricity in one of our state's leading institutions. He was bound to his position by strong ties, and his death came as a sudden shock."

Most of us have things or people in our past that we wish were not there. These are things that are an embarrassment to us, and we wish we could just do away with them. Of course, we have different choices as to what we can do with them.

1.   We can just pretend they don't exist. We can simply tell them to go away and act like they never really happened.

2.   We can always blame them on someone else. They really did happen, but it was not our fault so someone else will have to suffer the consequences for them.

3.   We can push them in the background of our minds and say, "I will take care of them in the future."

4.   We can place them before Him who invited us to seek and find; Him who taught us to pray, "forgive us our trespasses."

Ladies' Compliments

At a certain church there were two ladies who had unique ways of complimenting the preacher and song leader. One always said to the song leader, "Oh, you have such a mellow voice." The other lady always told the preacher, "Reverend, that was such a warm sermon." After hearing these same comments for quite some time, the preacher and the song leader decided to look in the dictionary to see exactly what these ladies were saying. They found that the lady who told the song leader that he had such a mellow voice was saying that his voice was over-ripe and nearly rotten, and the lady who told the preacher that his sermon was warm was saying that it wasn't so hot.

All of us enjoy hearing words of encouragement. We love to hear words that make us feel that we are having a positive influence on others. They make us feel successful. Oh, but let us remember that we should never put our total dependency on what others think. Yes, it's good to know that people think well of you, but teaching and preaching and speaking should be done for the glory of God. We never know who will be touched by what we say or do. Our spoken words are left at the feet of Jesus, and it is up to the Holy Spirit to use them to touch the hearts of people who need them.

Young Preacher as a Teacher

A young minister just out of seminary got his first job as a chaplain in a penitentiary. One of the first things he was asked to do was accompany a prisoner on his walk to the electric chair. As they walked along, the young chaplain wondered what he should say to the man. He couldn't say, "Good luck." He didn't want to say, "I'll see you in the morning." So he put his arm around him and said, "More power to you."

Words are very poor tools with which to express our feelings. We are told that there are over eight thousand words in our language. Most of us use about five thousand. However, when it comes to expressing what needs to be said, words often fall short. This is when a good handshake, a look of love, or a pat on the back convey as much or more than any verbal expression could. When we come to Robinsonville United Methodist Church and worship together, we convey to each other words of encouragement that help us overcome the problems we face in life.

The Frustrated Teacher 📖

A lady was filling in for a friend who kept a nursery with about twenty small children. She looked down at this little boy who was walking around barefoot on the cold floor. He had in his hand a pair of boots. She grabbed him up and began to try to put those boots on his feet. She pulled and pulled and almost never got them zipped, but when they were zipped, he looked up at her and said, "Dem ain't my boots." She began to work to get them off. She pulled and twisted; she broke both thumbnails getting them unzipped. When she got them off, he looked at her and said, "Dem are my sister's boots, and I'm supposed to wear dem."

Talk about frustration! However, there are so many things in life that frustrate us out of our wits. Just driving down the road, drivers do things that frustrate us. On our jobs where we work, things happen that literally frustrate us out of our wits. People in government today are very frustrating to all of us. In fact, things people in New York or California do can frustrate us. That is, if we allow ourselves to be frustrated.

A Preacher Oversleeps

A preacher had an early morning speaking appointment. He had set the clock to alarm at an appointed time, but for some reason the clock did not alarm. This put him fifteen minutes late. He went running into the bathroom to shave, he cut himself, and almost never got the bleeding stopped. When he finished dressing, he went running to the car, and he had a flat tire. Then he learned that the jack did not work right, but finally got the tire changed and backed out into the street and took off. He came to a four way stop sign and just went right through it. There was a policeman who ordered him out of the car. The preacher jumped out and said, "Alright officer, go ahead and give me a ticket, everything else has gone wrong today. The clock didn't alarm. I cut myself. The jack didn't work! Yes, just make my day a 100 percent lousy day." The officer very softly said, "Yes, I understand, before I became a Christian, I used to have days like that."

Isn't it amazing how things can happen to us that remind us that this is not a perfect world? Things go wrong at the right time to remind us that we are always in need of God's grace. Life simply is not perfect, and through His grace we must learn to take life as it comes to us, and in His power and guidance He will get us to our appointed place on time. This way we can save our temper. We might need it some day.

Secret Meetings 📖

O ur opportunities to witness come in strange ways. Here is why we should keep in touch with the Spirit of God. When Ruth and I retired, we built our house at the end of a street of a new subdivision. Ours was the only building in the area. At the end of the street behind us was about one hundred acres of heavily wooded area. There was just a wagon trail through the area. One afternoon I was working in my garden, and I noticed this man in a pickup truck go out into those woods a ways and stop. In a few minutes, a lady drove out to where he was, and this man got out of his truck and got in the car with her. It was evident that they knew each other because they were soon arm in arm, so I decided to go down and welcome them. I walked up behind the car on the man's side and I said, "Are you people interested in buying one of these lots?" The man said, "No." I said, "These are mighty fine lots, and we love living here." I almost walked away, but I turned back and said, "You know, I think it's absolutely wonderful that a husband and wife can come out here at the close of a busy day and admire God's handiwork in nature and to hear God speak through nature. You know, God does go out of His way to show us and to say to us, 'I love you.' And I am sure that after coming here and hearing God speak to you, your relationship at home with your children is much, much better. I think your kids are happy for you to come here and just talk with God."

All the time I was talking the man was tapping me on my arm saying, "Hey, say," but I kept talking. Then I said, "I wish you both God's blessings." I had not gone half-way back to the house when I heard them leave. I often wondered how things were at home. I never saw them come back again.

But this is not the end of this story. Some ten years later I was standing in Wal-Mart, and a man walked up to me and said, "Say, aren't you that preacher who lives in that Germanwood subdivision?" I said, "Yes, I am." He said, "Well, I've been wanting to say 'thanks' to you for saving my family. I am that guy who was in that car out in the woods behind your house. After you left us, I got to thinking about what you said, and I broke that relationship off, and I just want to thank you." He walked away. I have no idea who the man was, but I know this, God uses us when we allow Him to do so.

The Prayers We Pray 📖

A preacher friend of mine who served as a pastor in the North Carolina mountains told about calling on this elderly fellow to lead in prayer. Evidently, the old man felt that he had to inform God about all the happenings up there, so he told God about one fellow's sick cow, another fellow's coon dog that was caught in a trap, and so-and-so's sick baby and what was wrong with it. He told God about how dry it had been and that ponds were drying up and the grass was dying. Then he said, "And Lord, there are people dying up here that ain't never died before."

If we think about the kind of prayer life we have, don't you think some of us come pretty close to praying the same kind of prayer? Some of us are better at telling God about the wrongs of the world than we are at listening to Him tell us what He knows about us. If we confessed our problems and our needs, then that would lead to a whole new way of thinking for us. No, it's not easy for us to think about the wrongs in our lives, but our prayers should begin with us. Remember, we do not have to inform God about our world, nor about us. We begin by confessing and asking Him, "Forgive us our trespasses as we forgive those who trespass against us."

It Pays to be Honest 📖

There was this lady who lived under the philosophy that it always pays to be honest. She was forever and always saying in every situation, "You know, it pays to be honest." One day she and a friend got on a street car, and when she got to the back of the bus, she turned to her friend and said, "Oh, I must go back and pay my fare. It pays to be honest, you know." So, she went to pay her fare and when she returned, she smiled and said, "See, I told you it pays to be honest. I went up there and gave the man a dollar and he gave me change for a five."

This is what they call in the business, "Honesty for a price." Why do we obey the law? Is it because we are afraid of the penalties we might face if we are caught breaking the law, or is it because we believe it is the right thing to do? Why do people go to church? Some go because they think it helps them get to heaven. Some go because they think it is the right thing to do. Some go because it is a social function, and still others go to make business contacts. I attend church to receive strength and support from fellow Christians. I attend church because that is where God meets me as a part of His church, and I can contribute to whatever He is doing in my community and the world.

Roots

hanks for my roots. As I look back to my beginning life on earth, I am thankful that I was allowed to be born into the home of Walter and Kitty Cox Wood who were two hard-working (without many earthly riches), very religious persons. Walter and Kitty were parents of ten children, all of whom were fairly normal and of average intelligence. Of course, as a large family, we learned to share and to do without and to do necessary work.

I am also thankful that I was taught the value of church. We were taught to read music at a very young age. We didn't go to the doctor for every sore throat, but there was a home cure for everything. For a bad cold or a sore throat, it was Vick's salve. For other ailments, it was something else. Mom was our doctor for everything. After we all left home and something happened, she would tell us how to treat ourselves. If you got a splinter or briar in the foot, it was the same thing. Put a strip of fat meat on it, and it would draw the briar or splinter out. When I was pastor at Corinth, I was walking around the new fellowship part and stepped on a board that had a nail in it. The nail went right through my foot, shoe and all. The workmen on the job pulled the nail out and we put some rubbing alcohol and a bandage on the foot. That night I called Mom to see how she was doing, and I told her about the nail and like a flash she said, "Now, son, you put a biscuit and buttermilk poultice on that to draw the poison out." And I just said, "Well, Mom, what if I eat the biscuit and drink the buttermilk?" (I was glad she was thirty miles away.) She scolded me good and informed me how many times she had used it, and it *did* work.

Yes, I am thankful for the love our family had. That love was our greatest possession. We shared everything in work, play, and worship. I often think of the time Mom was going to Corinth with me for one night only. We had gone through the house and closed the windows and doors. As we came out the front door, she gave me a note to pin on the door. The note read, "THE KEY IS UNDER THE RUG." When I asked why she was doing that she looked at me as if I was not very bright. She said "Some of the other kids might come by and want in." You see, she didn't own anything that she valued more than her kids getting in if they came that way. They knew that the teacakes were on the table.

No, I do not go to the gravesite very often, but when I do, I love to go alone. Then I can stand quietly and think of Dad, the best man I have ever known, and Mom, and I remember that key under the rug and that biscuit and buttermilk poultice and say, "Thanks for your love."

Texas Farmer in Mississippi

This fellow from Texas was traveling across north Mississippi and grew tired and needed to stretch his legs. He saw this old Mississippi farmer standing beside the road, and he decided to stop and chat for a while. They visited a while, and the man from Texas asked the Mississippi fellow what he did in Mississippi. He said, "I farm." "Do you own your own farm?" the Texan asked. "Yep," said the Mississippian. "How big is your farm?" asked the Texan. The Mississippian said, "Well, it goes down to that tree in the hollow, and across to that tree on top of the hill, and back here. That is my farm." The Mississippian said, "And what do you do in Texas?" "Oh, I farm," replied the Texan. "Do you own your own farm?" asked the Mississippian. "Yep," said the Texan. "And how big is your farm?" asked the man from Mississippi. The Texan began, "Well, the best way I know to tell you is that the other morning I went out and got in my pickup and started driving at six o'clock in the morning, and I had not driven around my farm by seven o'clock that night." The old Mississippian said, "Do you know something, I used to have an old truck just like that!"

Some people simply are not impressed by the bigness of others' things. I think that is the way it should be. If we get all excited by every ounce of bigness that comes by us in life, we will be constantly moving from this to that. You see, just knowing who we are in the sight of Christ is enough for me. Let us remember that we are responsible to God for the amount God has given us.

Is It Tilly or Milly? 📖

This fellow married a lady named Tilly and they lived together ten years, had four children, and Tilly died. He took her out to the cemetery and buried her. Two years passed, and he met and married a lady named Milly. They lived together ten years, they had four children, and she took sick and died. He took her out to the cemetery and buried her, leaving a place between his two wives for his burial. A few years passed, and he took sick, and the doctor told him to get his estate in order because he did not have long to live. Therefore, he divided everything equally between the two sets of children. He called the eight kids in, and he said to them, "Now, I want both sets of children to know that I loved Milly and Tilly equally. There was not an ounce of difference between them, and I want you to bury me exactly between them, not one inch difference." They promised him that this would happen. Then the old man wrote a note to the undertaker telling him what he had done. He added, "Now confidentially, just between me and you, tilt me a little toward Tilly."

This is just another X-rated story because it's so far out, and yet we often find ourselves pulled between political opinions, business deals, and financial deals. There is one area of life, however, where we do not have a choice without it costing us. This is in the area of our commitment to God and His Church. The Ten Commandments are still the same today as they were thousands of years ago. The "thou shalt nots" are still the same and so are the "thou shalts."

In some areas, denominations get divided, and they divide the community. When people get together and talk about denomination, they are talking about things that divide, but when we talk about Jesus, we are talking about Him who unites us.

Pulling Hair Hurts 📖

This little four-year-old boy was playing in a room with his little one-year-old sister. All of a sudden he cried aloud, and the mother came and said, "What happened?" The little boy said, "My sister pulled my hair." The mother said, "Well, she doesn't know that it hurts when she pulls your hair." She then went back into the other room. She heard the little girl scream aloud, came back, and said, "What happened?" The little boy said, "She knows now."

It is a fact that some of the greatest lessons we learn in life come with some pain. My mom was a master at teaching her ten children how important this lesson was. Every time she paddled us, she gave a speech saying, "I love you, and because I love you, you must suffer this pain as a reminder that if you disobey, there will be some pain." I confess that I do understand the feeling of pain she was talking about.

It is in this same sense that we learn some great lessons about life. For example, life can get tough as we go through deep valleys or up steep mountainsides. But, is this not one of the ways we learn to trust God? Is not this how we learn that God is able to do all things for us that we need in life?

Someone has written a song that says something like this, "I do not pray that all the rough places in the road of life be removed and that my road be nothing but smooth travel. I just ask for grace and strength to overcome. And I will overcome with Him by my side."

Let us be thankful for all pain that draws us closer to Him.

God's Will and Milkshakes

There was a fellow who was a severe diabetic, but he liked milkshakes. One hot July afternoon, he was on his way home from work, and he wanted a milkshake in the worst way. So he decided to pray about it. He prayed this prayer: "Lord, if it is alright for me to have a milkshake today, let there be an empty parking place right in front of the front door of the ice cream parlor, and by this I will know that it won't hurt me." So he drove to the ice cream parlor, and sure enough, the tenth time around the block, there was the empty parking place.

All of us are guilty at times of this kind of praying. There are times when we are so vague that we are not sure of what we want ourselves. Sometimes our prayers are telling God what we want and even how He should answer our prayers. We have a way of answering our own prayer before we even listen to see what He thinks.

In order for us to have a successful prayer life, we need to make sure that we understand our request fully and that our prayer is not some vague request that we're not even sure of ourselves. If we're to have a successful prayer life we must ask God about His will for us, have plenty of time to listen, and expect Him to answer in His way. There are times when God says, "Yes." And sometimes, "No." Sometimes He says, "wait a while."

His answer is always best for us.

Thirty

Twenty-Five Cents Too Much For a Wedding?

Back forty years ago, I got to know this ninety-year-old preacher who told about doing a wedding around the turn of the century. He said the couple came, and he did the wedding, and when he finished, the boy said, "Preacher, how much do I owe you?" The preacher said, "Oh, whatever you think it's worth." Then the boy gave him a quarter. The preacher said he looked at the girl and gave the boy fifteen cents back. However, to that boy she must have been beautiful. Who can judge beauty; what is beauty? No two of us agree.

Now that is quite a story, but let's just hope and think the boy got a bargain that we do not see on the surface. Maybe she was the best cook in the countryside. Maybe she was the finest housekeeper of any country girl in the area. On the other hand, maybe she was the best mother for his children to be found in the whole area. Maybe she was just the best wife to him that he could ever have found. As the years passed by, there was a sweetness about her that was not found in every wife. She was a tremendous manager of the household. In just a short time, old Jim began to count his blessings in that wife of his. When they came to their golden years of marriage he could say every day, "My, what a bargain I have." After all, beauty is as beauty does, and beauty is only skin deep.

They Both Jump 📖

A man was standing on this bridge banister about ready to jump off to his death when a passing policeman saw him, stopped, and pleaded with him not to jump. The policeman said, "Just think of all your blessings." The fellow said, "Let me tell you, my wife left me. She took my life's savings to give to another man. I am broke. My children have all turned against me. My friends have denied me. My job is gone. I am a nobody in my church and community." So, they both jumped.

I suppose there are times when the easy thing to do would be just jump off a bridge and end it all. Back in the Old Testament times the Psalmist said, "Oh that I could take wings and fly away." Jonah was so fearful of his future that he ran away from it. All these were easy ways out but not the best way.

The best way to face any problem is to hold the hand of Him who is our victory. Any time we feel that we are failures in life we can turn to Him, and He reminds us of His victory on the cross. One of the greatest contemporary gospel songs that we all love is entitled, "Victory in Jesus." We can all sing this song.

The Boy Thinks Big 📖

A father had been teaching his little son that he should always think positive about everything, that he should always think BIG. The little boy had a puppy that he wanted to sell. So he made a sign and put it in the yard. It said, "Puppy for sale $1.00." When the father came home from work, he said, "Son, you can't sell that dog like that, you've got to think big." The next day the boy had his sign read, "Puppy for sale $100.00." When the father came home, the sign and puppy were gone. The father said, "Son, did you sell the dog for $100.00?" The son answered, "Yes, but I had to take two $50.00 cats for it."

This story reminds us that not all bargains are that big. The advertisement world tries to make us feel that a certain item is the best bargain around. In the super malls, a sale sign is on everything. Of course, one has to be careful and know the value of everything one buys.

In the moral and spiritual world, the lights are flashing and a thing might look good, but again, one has to be aware of the value of life itself. We must ask: What eternal value to my life does this have?

Again, let us remember that some bargains are not bargains. Church time worship is always good and gives us all that we bargain for.

A Preacher's Repeat 📖

A preacher went to fill in for a friend who was a pastor of a middle-sized church. At the close of the service, members were coming by, shaking the preacher's hand and congratulating him. However, this one fellow came through the line and he said, "Reverend, you preached too long." He came back through and said, "Reverend, you preached too loud." He came back a third time and said, "What you said did not amount to anything." A deacon came to him and said to the preacher, "Sir, I do not know what that man coming through the line has said to you, but let me say, he is not all there. He does not even know what to say. The only thing he ever knows to say is what he hears other people say."

No matter who we are, one of the most dangerous things we can do is to repeat a "they say." From the time Jesus began His public ministry until Calvary, He suffered from hundreds and hundreds of "they says." "They says" can be costly to any of us. "They says" can come from anybody and can be oh-so-ill-advised. There is a policy that is good for us to follow. It is this: If you cannot say something good about someone, do not say it. In the Bible, this is called "gossip" and is very evil. There is enough good to be said about anyone to last us from one Sunday till the next. We can take this as the Spirit's mark of kindness.

Different Views 📖

wo ladies met on the street and one said to the other, "My, what have you done to your hair? Why, it looks like a wig." The other lady said, "Well, it *is* a wig." The other one responded by saying, "Well, you can't tell it by looking."

There is nothing new about some people having nothing to say, and they say it. Some of us get the idea sometimes that we just have to say something when we do not. When we do not have anything to say, and we say it, we are merely word sayers. In the New Testament, Simon Peter was always and forever doing this to Jesus. When he had nothing to say, he said it, and it always got him into trouble. When they were up there on the Mount of transfiguration witnessing that great moment, one of the greatest moments in human history, he said something that didn't make sense.

Have you ever asked yourself how many of the words we blurt out in some holy moment really don't mean anything? How much better off we would be if we just sat in silence and meditation and listened to the man of Galilee and to what He wants to say and do for us? When people have nothing to say and say it within the circle of family and friends, are we not in danger of saying something about someone that might hurt or harm their reputation and standing in the church and community? Careless words can destroy friendships that can take years to repair. Careless words are very difficult to reclaim. Yes, we are at our best when in worship at church.

Imagination

lady said to her husband, "Honey, what do you admire most about me? Is it my brilliant mind, my bubbling outgoing personality, or is it my beautiful face and body?" Without hesitation the man said, "Oh, honey, the thing I admire most about you is your exaggerating imagination."

Oh, isn't it something that some people just never seem to get around to learning the truth about themselves? It is a terrible thing to think you are someone else. Oh, you have the right name, but you do not fit that name. Being two people will eventually destroy any of us. Being someone else can destroy who we are now and who we will become in the future. We have all read the story of Dr. Jekyll and Mr. Hyde. Because Dr. Jekyll did not destroy that hideous beast when he could destroy him, then the beast destroyed him. Knowing who we are, knowing that we are creatures of God, and knowing that we are loved and that we are valuable to Him, is important. Church is a place where we know ourselves. It is a place where we gain strength. Church is the place where we gain spiritual food and where we learn the truth about who we are and who our fellowman is.

Elevator

There was this old man who had never seen a high rise building and therefore knew nothing about elevators. Finally, he came to town and was standing beside this tall building when all of a sudden the wall just opened up and a little old lady with a walking stick walked into that hole, and then it just closed up on her. He kept standing there trying to figure out what had happened to her when the wall opened up again. This time a beautiful young blond came walking out of that hole. His remarks were, "Well, I be dagone, that beats anything I have ever seen. I sure wish my old woman could get in that thing."

One of the things that we humans are good at is seeing the needs of others. However, we are weak at seeing our own needs. This is just a story and a tall tale, but this old man probably needed to get in that thing as much or more than the old woman. As we see others' weaknesses, maybe we should make it a practice of looking at ourselves before we say anything. Now, where this story really comes into play is in our religion. The Bible tells us that Jesus encountered people like this. They strained at a gnat and swallowed a camel. They worked at getting a splinter out of their neighbor's eye but had a two-by-four in their own. Going to church and worshipping helps us look at ourselves. Kneeling at the communion table helps us see our own needs. Just think how great it could have been if the old man could have walked in and come out clean and dressed up and gone home to his wife a whole new person. It could have led her to come running to get in also. Maybe his children would have come with her.

Teeth Are Important

An old couple, celebrating their fiftieth wedding anniversary, were sitting out in the yard under a shade tree. She was sitting on the swing, he was in a chair, and they were saying very little. Finally, she said, "Pa, why don't you come and sit beside me like you used to?" He got up, went over and sat beside her. After a while she said, "Pa, why don't you sit close to me and put your arm around me like you used to?" Therefore, he did. Then she said, "Pa, why don't you bite me on my ear and tickle my neck like you used to?" He got up and walked toward the house. She said, "Pa, where are you going?" He said, "To get my teeth."

Love is expressed in many different ways. Love grows with years. The bonds of love grow stronger with years of experience. Mature love is expressed with a look, with a shared responsibility, in the name: Pa, Ma, Jim, Mary, the pet way of calling a name. This love is seen in the way one gets their favorite piece of chicken and the other one gets theirs. Love is seen in the special way of doing little things for each other.

When God instituted the family, as valuable as words are, and as much as "I LOVE YOU" means to each one, it's the little things we learn to do for each other that makes lovers living together a thing of joy and home like the place we call Heaven. Words are fine, but deeds last longer. Yes, getting the teeth does help. Church is important in bringing husband and wife closer to God and to each other.

Crown of Stars 📖

here is a story about this town that had three churches on Main Street. On Sunday morning as you drove down the street, the first church was singing, "Will there be any stars in my crown." As you came to the second church, they were singing, "No, not one." Then the third church was singing, "And that will be glory for me."

Now, I have not told this story to get a laugh. In fact, I did not tell it to get a grin. You see, I think it's awful when we fight and say hurtful things against other groups of Christians over man-made issues. It is my belief that most denominational groups were brought into the world by God for a purpose in that day and in that place. God is still working through them all.

Oh, if we could all remember that when we talk about man-made issues, we are talking about things that divide us. But when we talk about Christ and the Holy Spirit, we talk about Him who unites us. Let us remember that we are all on the same team.

Bandaged Ears

There was this fellow who went to work, and he had both ears bandaged. Someone asked him what had happened to his ears. And he said, "Well, last night I was ironing and the phone rang, I thought I was picking up the phone, but it was the iron." They said, "Well, what happened to the other ear?" He said, "Well, I got that ear bandaged and went back to ironing with the other hand, and would you believe that fool called again."

And that tale is just another one of those far-out stories. However, we have all done some of those foolish and dumb things. Yes, we have done a few ridiculous things when our minds were miles and miles away, like drive right through a stop sign. Why, we have even said things that if we had just thought about who it might hurt, we would never have said them. Yes, we have done some foolish things, like neglect to read the Bible. How foolish. We have neglected to pray when we needed to listen to Him, but we foolishly went our own way thinking that it would not hurt anything. We have foolishly neglected to tell our mate, "Honey, I love you." We did not think it would matter, but it did. We neglected church, and we did not think it would matter, but it did. It mattered to that youngster who watched our foolish ways, and in the end, it mattered to us.

Marriage with Nothing 📖

everal years ago, I had an elderly couple that married when she was fifteen, and he was seventeen. They had reared fourteen children, all of whom were married, had their own families, and had all done well. In visiting them, I often found them sitting on the couch, holding hands. Many times they told me that they started housekeeping with one bed, two chairs, a stove, a cow, and a mule. Their children were schoolteachers, public officials, and successful business people. However, as we talked about their meager beginning, the old fellow would always say to me, "Brother Huey, me and my ole lady started out with nothing, and sixty years later we still have most of it."

Of course, we always laughed and knew that he was joking. From this we would always count some of their blessings and their riches. We would think of these children and grandchildren. We would always say that they would not have taken a million dollars for them. We would talk about how they had been blessed in having good health through these years, about these fourteen children and the fact that none of them had been issued a police ticket for anything. All their fourteen families were active in church. However, the thing that he boasted about the most was that their names had not been tarnished in any way. All were honest, upright citizens. On top of all this, their Christian names were as clean and pure as they had ever been. By now my friends were both smiling because they knew that they were rich.

The old couple may have started with nothing, but when I visited them, I was aware that they were rich. They always said, "We could not have made it without the church and God."

Sam and Prosperity

A young preacher moved into a new community and had been there about a week when he started to look over the church roll. He found this man's name and beside it someone had written "inactive." Therefore, the young preacher decided to go see this man. It was no trouble to find Sam; he lived right out at the edge of town in a small cottage. The young preacher asked him why he did not attend church. Sam said, "Well, I will just tell you, I don't have clothes to wear. The only shoes I have are these with holes in them." The young preacher felt sorry for him, and he went back to the church and got some money out of this account and that one. He went and bought the man new shoes, a new shirt, new suit, new tie, and everything to go with it and took them to Sam. Sunday came, and the young preacher was looking for Sam at church, but he was not there. Monday he went to see Sam and asked him why he did not come to church. And Sam said, "Preacher, I put that new shirt, suit, tie, and shoes on, and I looked in the mirror at myself. I looked so prosperous that I decided to go to the Episcopal Church."

It is strange how a little prosperity can affect some people's loyalty. It is also true that so many little things affect our loyalty. A simple thought that someone else has a little more land or a finer automobile or more of this or that can keep us from seeking the better things of life. I can't tell you if having on a new shirt, suit, and shoes made any difference with Sam's receiving the spirit of God. I don't think so, but worrying and being concerned about his looks certainly kept him from many blessings. Wouldn't it be wonderful if we all learned the art of looking more at the spirit of other people and less at their social standings in the community? Wouldn't it be great if Sam would have remembered who he was, a child of God? *That* is who we are, and *that* is what counts most.

Snoring Dog and Husband 📖

A lady had a dog that snored, and one night she went to bed but could not go to sleep because the dog was snoring. Someone told her that if she would tie a red ribbon on the dog's ear, it would stop it from snoring. She got up, found a red ribbon, tied it on the dog's ear, stopped the snoring, and she went back to sleep. Then her good husband came in, went to bed, and he began snoring. She decided to try putting a ribbon on his ear. She could not find another red ribbon but found a blue one. She put it on his ear. It stopped the snoring, and she went to sleep. The next morning she got up, went to work, and left the two sleeping. Finally, the fellow awoke, raised up, and felt that ribbon on his ear. He pulled it off and looked at it. He then looked at the dog with the ribbon on its ear, and he said, "Buster, I do not know where we went last night or what we did, but we won first and second place!"

Determination is a wonderful thing to have so long as it is directed to good things for life. When I think of all the good things wrought by sheer determination, I am reminded of the electric light bulb. Or, I think of the airplane or the medicine used to heal the many diseases that no longer threaten life. These were brought about because someone was determined to win.

How about our spiritual lives? Will we be determined like Saint Paul, that we shall be true to our vows in marriage, that we will be parents and grandparents worthy of our calling? Let us determine to be good examples to all youth around us by daily walking in His steps.

Surprised

here is a story about the fellow who came back to his hometown after being away for several years. He was walking down the street and met this lady he had known back years ago. They talked a minute, and the fellow said, "By the way, how is your husband Jim doing?" She said, "Oh, since I last saw you, Jim slipped away into Heaven." The man almost said, "Oh, I am sorry," but he could not say that. She might think he was sorry Jim went to Heaven. Then he almost said, "I am glad." However, he could not say that either. She might think he was glad Jim was dead. So, he simply said, "I am surprised."

It's tough being a prisoner to words. With all the words we have access to, we sometimes find ourselves with nothing to say. Even the word *thanks* falls short and at times sounds empty. The same is true with the expression I love you. How do we tell our mate of fifty years or more, "I love you, and I appreciate you?" Does it mean what the heart feels and you do not? When we think of all that our Lord has done and continues to do for us (He gives us the air we breathe, the health we have, the family, the friends, the land plus the hope we have in tomorrow and eternity) how can we say, "I love you" and mean what our hearts feel? It's here that coming to church and worshipping with other members of His family in love speaks what He enjoys hearing. Oh, I would not miss it for anything. It is good for me to know that my life speaks what I want to say.

She Can See To Drive at Night 📖

T wo old fellows had not seen each other for some eight or nine years. After talking a while John said to Jim, "Jim, since I last saw you, my wife died, and I have married again." Jim said, "Well, is she good looking?" "No," said John, "she really isn't." "Well, is she a good cook?" "No," said John, "she really can't cook a lick. In fact I do all the cooking." "Well, does she have a lot of money?" Jim asked. "No," said John. "In fact she was on welfare when we married." "Then why did you marry her?" asked Jim. John replied, "Well, you see, she can see to drive at night."

Now, even though this is just a tall tale and a far-out story, and one that we would not recommend for grounds to marry, doesn't it sort of match the signs of our time? Doesn't it speak on the issue of holy matrimony when it is taken so lightly? Holy marriage is a bond between a man and a woman, and it is recorded in Heaven in a bond of love. Marriage is not an agreement that can be broken because someone simply decides that it is suddenly not for them. Holy marriage in family relationship is like the bond of Christ and His church.

What this story really is saying to us is that marriage is a serious business and is more than a contract to be taken lightly. Marriage is a social and spiritual bond, and home is a place of unity and respect.

Church worship and home worship are both very important.

The Procrastination Club 📖

I learned the other day that a new procrastination club has been organized. The cost for yearly membership is one hundred dollars. The club headquarters is Dallas, Texas, which gives it a central location. The club does not have a name yet, but a committee was appointed to come up with a classy name. This committee was appointed three years ago, but each year the members have requested another year for their study.

Members were to get a lot for their one hundred dollars. For example, this year the meeting was scheduled for November. Members were to get two days and nights of free lodging, free meals, and a free ticket to a Dallas Cowboys' game. That is quite a bargain. However, the meeting for this year of 2001 has been put off until next November.

Most of us are guilty of procrastination. We put off visiting an elderly person until it is too late. We put off calling a friend just to say "I care" until the friend feels that we don't. We put off saying "I'm sorry" until a relationship is strained. We put off saying "I love you" until someone dear is hurt. We put off going to church until we feel some pressing need. We put off asking God's forgiveness until we can see ourselves as the unwholesome creatures we are. We often put off acknowledging our need for the Savior until we become spiritual and sometimes physical paupers. But Christ patiently waits with sufficient love for all His children.

Life in a Monastery 📖

A fellow who was all fed up with life in general was walking by a monastery and decided to take a look at the inside. All of the monks living inside seemed to be at peace. Life, for him, living on the outside was not good. So, he decided to go in and see if they would take him. He did— and they did. The rules were that he could remain a full year and at the end of the year, he could say two words. After the second year, he could say two more words, and at the end of the third year he could say two more. At the end of the first year he said, "Bed hard." At the end of the second year he said, "Food bad." After the third year he said, "I quit." At this the head monk replied, "Well, you might as well. All you've done since coming here is gripe, gripe, gripe."

One of the things that we could say of poor old Judas is that he had it made and didn't know it. Here he is with Jesus, a trusted disciple who could be counted in the loyal circle of Jesus. He had it made and didn't know it.

We too are a part of the most blessed people in the whole world. We have more material things; we have more political freedom than any other people in the world. We live in the land of the open Bible. We have freedoms that other people only hear about. We live in this land of free democracy with all the food and clothing we could possibly want, yet we still have problems. We must face them in prayer and dedication, and the church is where we begin.

The White Rabbit 📖

A fellow moved into a new community where there was a lady who lived behind him who had a beautiful white rabbit that she kept in a small pen in her backyard. He owned a great big Doberman dog. He knew that, given the chance, his dog would kill the rabbit. So he built a high fence that he knew his dog couldn't climb over. Afterward, he went to work feeling at ease.

Two days later, he came home and there his dog stood in the backyard with that rabbit in his mouth, all dirty and dead. He just knew his dog had gotten under the fence and killed the rabbit. He thought, "I must do something about this." So he took the rabbit and shampooed it and took some fine wire and fixed the rabbit so it would stand up like it was alive and put it back inside the neighbor's fence. In a couple of hours, he heard this lady scream at the top of her voice, and he climbed to the top of the fence and asked what the lady's problem was. She said, "My rabbit died yesterday, and I dug a hole here in the yard. When I buried it, it was all dirty, but here it is white, alive, and cleaner than it has ever been."

Now, I can't tell you about this story, but this I know— things do sometimes come alive when they've been dead. We've seen this happen to communities; we've seen it happen to businesses; we've seen it happen to churches and groups of people. We have seen it happen to individuals. Homes die, then come alive. Have you ever read this: "Wherein I once was dead—and now I am alive"? It does happen! A person comes to church, and they have no life, they are lifeless, but after a touch of real friendship, a touch of the Master's hand, they are alive.

Looks Kill 📖

here was this mountain lady sitting on a stump far back up in the hills. By her side was this pile of squirrels. A game warden walked up and said, "Lady, are these your squirrels?" "Yep," she replied. "Then give me your gun," he said. "You have killed more than the limit." She said, "I ain't got no gun." "Then how did you kill these squirrels?" he asked. She said, "I just make an ugly face at them, and they fall out." The warden didn't believe her, but they looked up in a tree and saw a squirrel. She made a face, and it fell out. "How did you learn to do that?" the warden asked. "My husband showed me how," she said. "Does he still kill squirrels this way?" asked the warden. She said, "No, Pa got to where he tore 'em up too bad."

Before we turn this story off as being too ridiculous and too far out, let's remind ourselves that some of the faces we create do have the capacity to kill something inside us or inside someone else.

A greedy face can kill any hope of friendship.

A jealous face can kill a love that exists between two lovers.

A superior face can kill any hope of brotherhood or sisterhood.

A haughty face can kill the spirit of worship.

HOWEVER

A smiling face restores friendships.

A joyful face restores trust.

A peaceful and gentle face restores confidence.

A kind face restores respectability.

A loving, God-like face produces worship and praise.

If you are looking for those good faces that lead us to new life, then worship with us.

Real Love 📖

little kindergarten boy came home from school and announced that he had a new sweetheart. "Does she love you?" Dad asked. The little boy said, "I don't know, but she do like she do."

Oh, the wisdom of a little child. Oh, now I know that there are so many things that this little child did not understand about love. There is that time element and other things that he didn't understand, but, "She do like she do" is a good beginning mark of love. If you move up the ladder of age to teenage and beyond, it means respect for who they are, what they are, and what they will be in the future. Real love will not take advantage of love in a way that will bring a guilty conscience later in life. Real love will not change its mind with popularity.

I walked into a business in our town one day and there were three young girls working the cash register, and the one in the middle had the attention of the other two. She was saying, "Have you girls heard that Angie has fallen madly in love with the new boy in school? His name is Paul, and she is really in love." One of the other girls said, "I thought she was in love with Benny." "Oh, she was but not anymore." And the third girl said, "Well, what happened to Tommy? I thought she was in love with him." And the first girl said, "Oh, that was three months ago."

She had my change, and as she handed it to me, I just put my hands up to my very dirty and sweaty face and looked at her and asked, "Goodness, what do you think she is going to do when she sees me?"

The other two girls turned their backs because I don't think they wanted to laugh at me, but this one just smiled and never answered.

But this is what is called "puppy love," and we understand it. But real love not only acts and respects, but suffers
for love and supports that love. Yes, I am a firm believer in
the fact that if we love God and His church, then nothing
will keep us away from worship. Yes, we desire body contact
with our love and the same is true with our love for God and
the church.

Hurried Lives 📖

I f you were asked to describe this age with just one word, what word would you choose? After thinking of this for several days, I have settled on the four letter word: late. Now, why did I settle on this word? Well, if you will go with me up Germantown Road at 6:00 A.M. and watch how people drive to save five seconds you will see what I mean. One morning I was going to Saint Francis Hospital to be with the family of a man who was having surgery. On that street, there are three lanes going north and three lanes coming south. I was in the middle lane. On my right was a man who was driving recklessly trying to pass the car in front, but couldn't. We came to Shelby Drive and were the last who did not make the green light. In the car in the left lane was a young lady who looked to be in her late twenties. As we came to a stop, she grabbed her purse and out came her cosmetics. She did her lips first, and then she did her eyes, and then the face powder, then the hair brush. When she had finished with all of this, she put all that stuff back into her purse. Then she realized that someone might be watching, and she turned and looked at me. I gave her the big okay sign and nodded with a smile. By that time, the light turned green, and she took off ninety to nothing, gone out of my sight in nothing flat. As I drove along I wondered, "Why did she do her face here at that stop light?" Is it something she does every morning? Does she leave her house at a certain time every day so she can be here at this two minute light every day? Or did she make her face here today because the baby was sick this morning, and it just clung to Mommy saying, "Don't go, Mommy." Or is she late because she has a no-good fellow for a husband who never helps her get the kids ready for day care. No, I do not know why the lady did her face here at this stoplight. I just know that she did. What a shame that our time is spread that thin, and one wonders where a person can get time to study the scripture, pray to God, or visit a prospect for the church. Yes, one wonders.

Why Fire Trucks Are Red 📖

o you know why fire trucks are red? Well, because fire trucks have four wheels and eight men. Everybody knows that four and eight makes twelve. There are twelve inches in a foot. And a foot is a ruler. Queen Elizabeth, a ruler, is also the name of the largest ship on the seas. Seas have fish and fish have fins. The Finns fought the Russians. Russians are red. Fire trucks are always rushin'. Therefore, fire trucks are always red.

Now if you think this is wild, what must God think as He listens to people's reasoning for not attending worship services, Sunday school, and tithing? He sends sunshine and rain, and He blesses us with the greatest place on the face of the earth to live, and then people come with their silly excuses for failing to worship. That fire truck business makes more sense.

Now here's a thought for you: right is right if nobody does it. Wrong is wrong if everybody does it.

Shingles 📖

A fellow walked into a doctor's office and was greeted by a receptionist who asked him what he had. He said, "Shingles." She took his name and address and told him to wait. He waited thirty minutes and a nurse's aid came and asked him what he had. He said, "Shingles." She took his blood pressure and pricked his finger. She told him to go in a room and wait. He waited thirty minutes and a nurse came and asked him what he had. He said, "Shingles." She took blood and told him to take his shirt off and wait. He waited thirty minutes and the doctor came in and asked him what he had. He said, "Shingles." The doctor said, "Where?" He said, "They are out there on my truck. I am trying to find out where you want me to unload them."

With all our modern technology today, communication is still a major problem with us. One of the reasons for this is that we don't have time to listen. A friend can ask how you are doing and then doesn't have time to wait to hear what you say. We are told that our concentration length is getting shorter and shorter. If a sermon is more than twenty minutes long, members get restless. I say that our prayer line to God is the only clear line we have, and we have to work at keeping our end of the line open.

The most important time of our week is the time we come to worship on Sunday.

It's the only time we slow down and listen to God speak to us in the hymns, the prayers, and the reading of the scripture. Our communication with God is always an open line. God hears every whisper. He hears our blundering words and even a whisper. We never have to wait. Our prayer to Him is a direct call.

Fiftieth Anniversay 📖

ost of us have been guilty of doing or saying something on a sudden urge and felt that we were doing the right thing only to learn later that it was wrong. We have also done or said something on that sudden urge and learned later that it was the greatest thing we've ever done because that opportunity just may not have come our way again, and we would have lost that opportunity forever.

You might think of some experience like this in your past. You had just one opportunity to do it, and you responded to that sudden urge, and it became a great blessing to you and someone else also. Today you are so thankful that you acted on that sudden urge. This might be some small something like an act of kindness to a total stranger. It might be some small deed, but you felt an urge to do it, and it brought a feeling of joy and blessing to your life. This kind of thing can happen anywhere, even here at church. You have to say something to someone, and you do it, and it does something good for your life.

But for myself, I am thinking back several years ago when I had a sudden urge to do something that has changed my whole life forever. If I had not responded to my sudden urge, I just might not have had the opportunity again, and I would have been a terrible, terrible loser. Oh, and the thing about this act was that it took a whole lot of courage on my part. And what was my sudden urge? And why did it take courage? I asked a beautiful young lady, whom I had not seen but one time since childhood days, for a date. Had I failed to act on this sudden urge and not asked for a date, she would have gone on to MSCW, and I would have gone back to Jackson, Mississippi, and who knows what might have happened. But I would have been the loser. But the good news is, I responded to my urge. I asked, and it all leads to this good story.

So, today, I am forever thankful for that sudden urge, and I am thankful that I responded to it and asked this beautiful young lady (Ruth) for a date. Yes, if I had it to do over today, I'd do it again with joy.

Yes, God Does Speak 📖

A fellow said, "I hear you preachers talking about God speaking to them, calling them and all of this. I want you to know that I am religious and a member of the church, but I have never heard God speak to me, and I want to know what I need to do to get God to speak to me." The preacher said, "Well, let me suggest that on some stormy, rainy night you go out in your yard and you look up into the heavens and you ask God to speak to you. A couple of weeks passed and the fellow came back to see his minister and said, "Preacher, last night in that thunder-rainy storm I went outside just like you said, and I asked God to speak to me, but I did not hear God speak to me." The preacher said, "You mean that you did not hear a voice of any kind speak to you?" The fellow said, "The only voice I heard was that one that said, "You fool," and so I just went back into the house. The preacher then said, "Well, how much more do you want God to say to you in one night?"

Most of us have trouble hearing God speak because we never shut up our gabbing. It is just impossible to hear God when we are constantly letting our tongues get in front of our brains. Another truth is that God is a gentleman, and He will not force His way into our hearts. Oh yes, it is a truth that we have as much of Him as we bargain for. Yes, we call him into our hearts and minds, but He never forces His way into our hearts. He comes by invitation only.

Rough Ride

A Methodist preacher went to visit at this Baptist revival. They stayed and stayed, and finally they called on him to dismiss with prayer. He prayed, "Lord, I sure hate to wake you up at this late hour, but I just want to ask you to help us stay awake until we get home. Amen."

A Baptist preacher came to preach in a Methodist church. It was a hot summer day. The preacher preached and preached. There was a glass of water on the pulpit, and the preacher would take a drink every few minutes. He would preach some more and then get another drink of water. The preacher finally finished the sermon, and he turned to the Methodist pastor and asked if he had anything to say. He said, "Well, we were going to have a baptizing, but you've drunk our baptistry dry."

A lady had been on her first airplane trip. She wrote a letter complaining about her trip. She said that a sign would come on saying, "Fasten your seatbelt." She said that she noticed that every time that sign came on, the ride got rough, and she thought they should stop flashing that sign. This is an imperfect world, isn't it?

There was this lady who had been away from her home community for a few years. She came back for a visit and was grocery shopping and met a lady whom she had known years ago. In fact she did not know that the lady's husband had died two months ago, and she asked how he was feeling. The lady replied, "He is gone." The lady assumed that he had gone on a trip or something, and she said, "Well, why didn't you go with him?"

An English professor wrote the words, "Woman without her man is a savage." She directed the students to punctuate the sentence correctly. He found that the men looked at it one way and the women another. The women wrote, "Woman, without her, man is a savage." The men wrote, "Woman, without her man, is a savage."

Ladies' Day 📖

i f a man is alone in the woods, far back where nobody can hear him, and he makes a noise, and there is not a woman near enough to hear him, is he still wrong? Please forgive me, ladies. I really don't care for this kind of story.

Mr. Neely, one of my professors at Candler Theological Seminary, shared this poem for preachers who boast that they are original in what and how they preach:

He preachest best who stealeth best
From all things great and small.
For he who preachest best by far,
From nature stole it all.

This fellow took a job playing Santa Claus at a Sears store. He stood by the front door and said, "HO, HO, HO." He worked three days and was fired. He kept forgetting the words.

Two white corpuscles lived in a blood stream of a horse. They were doing quite well, but you know how this works. The grass always looks greener on the other side of the fence. So, they changed streams. But, as soon as they got there a red corpuscle came along and ate them up. Now the moral of this story is that you should never change streams in the middle of a horse.

A lady and her husband walked into a dentist's office, and the lady said to the girl at the desk, "I need to see the doctor right now. I need him to pull a tooth." The girl called the dentist. He came in, and she said, "Doctor, you've just got to pull this tooth now. The pain in unbearable, and we've got to go out of town this morning, and this pain is so great." The dentist said, "Well, it will take an hour for the shot to take effect." She said, "No, no we don't want a shot. I just want you to pull this tooth now, but no shot." The doctor said, "Well, which tooth is it?" She said. "Honey, show the doctor your tooth."

This mother rabbit would leave her two babies every morning and go out in search of food, but with these instructions: "Don't go into that valley. If you do a goon will catch you and eat you." But then they came to the time when they thought that they could do as they pleased. So, they took off to the valley and sure enough a goon caught them and ate them. And the moral of this story is that sometimes you're hare today and goon tomorrow.

Conclusion

*T*here was an elderly lady who would sometimes get happy and shout in church. Of course, this was an embarrassment to some members of her family. They never told her that she shouldn't shout, but they discouraged her anytime they could.

One night they were having a visiting evangelist preach at their church, and they knew that he was the type of preacher who could get Grandma excited. They also knew that Grandma loved beautiful quilts, and she had found one that she really liked and wanted. So one of the granddaughters said to her, "Grandma, if you are quiet at church tonight, and if you don't shout, I will give you that quilt that you've been wanting." Grandma accepted the deal.

Well, the worship service began that night with congregational singing. They sang some of her favorite songs, "Amazing Grace," "Rock of Ages," and "What a Friend," and Grandma sat as still as a mouse.

Then there were some people who stood to testify, and they told of how good God had been to them. Grandma sat as still and quiet as she could.

Then the preacher stood and read the Twenty-third Psalm. He also read John fourteen. Then he began to talk about the words of Jesus. The preacher said that Jesus was going to prepare a place for His own and that He would come back and take His own home with Him to live forever. Grandma had remained quiet and still, but her bucket was getting fuller and fuller. Then the preacher began talking about the beauty of heaven, and finally Grandma took her hat and waved it as high as she could and said as loud as she could, "Quilt or no quilt, praise the Lord!"

No, people don't shout today. I wonder why? Is it that they had something we don't have? Or is it that we know something that they didn't know?

But I wonder why?

Let's not forget that there is more than one way to shout. As for me, there have been many times while driving down the road, and I would be looking at the beauty of God's handiwork and thinking of all His blessings to me, the great churches I have served and how the people have loved me and done so much for me, I would call out as loud as I could, "PRAISE THE LORD. Thank you Lord." Then there were the times when I thought of my family and how proud I am of them, and I shouted, "Thank you, Lord."

But as I am coming to these last pages of this book, I realize how God has led me and given me the words. I think of how He has led me in collecting stories through the years and how He gave me the sermon "The Master's Watermelon Patch" at 3:00 A.M. I think that when the last word is written, I will say it so that all my neighbors can hear me shout, "Praise God from whom all blessings flow."

I also hope that when you have read these last words of this book, you will have been so blessed that you will stand and raise your eyes heavenward and say, "To God be the glory, great things He has done and is doing." Amen.

SCRIPTURE: I KINGS 20:40 "As thy servant was busy here and there the prisoner was gone." Now let's revisit the story about the young man and his watermelon.

A young man is sitting at a table in a small restaurant; his right hand is pushed tightly up into his armpit, and he is trying to eat his meal with his left hand. He is having all kinds of problems, and a little waitress comes up to him and says, "Sir, I am sorry that you are crippled like that." "Crippled? What do you mean? Crippled! I'm not crippled." She says, "I thought you were crippled with your hand up under your arm like that." He looks down at his hand, jerks his hand out, hits his forehead, and says, "Goodness gracious. I've lost my watermelon!"

Now when you read this story, it will bring a smile because it is so very ridiculous and far out. You see, such a thing could never happen. No one could lose a watermelon because watermelons are just too heavy and there is no way you wouldn't miss it. This young man said that he had lost his watermelon. But this is not the first time that some bright and intelligent youngster has been trudging down the road of life thinking all is well, and his life is secure, but then something happens, and the whole quality of his life just goes out the window. He has lost his watermelon. So, who am I to say that there is nothing to this watermelon story?

So, as we are thinking about this young man and his melon, we are reminded that watermelons have been lost before. Some of them were huge. We have all known someone who lost (of all things) their quality of life. Some have lost their most treasured possessions. And they didn't know they had lost it until it was needed.

So we come to ask ourselves this very personal question: What are our watermelons? We know this, we all have one. We know that it could be anything from our high and holy dreams for life. As parents, it may include all our church activities and worship habits. Why, it might include our vocations and our callings and our willingness to hear God when He calls us. All of these might well be our watermelons, and we are responsible for their safekeeping.

The point I am making here is that people lose things that are much bigger and much more difficult to handle than a watermelon. Of course, this leads me to see that a watermelon can be lost. In fact, as we look at the book of Genesis, we're reminded of all that Adam and Eve lost. Just think, they lost their dwelling place in paradise. I can't tell you how big that dwelling place was, but I'd guess that this watermelon was mustard seed in comparison to it. And do you know how they lost that time? Listening to idle, irresponsible advice. Man has always had false promises and empty advice on how to be happy in a world that he doesn't own. Now, I don't know, but it could have been that while this young man was listening to a lot of empty promises that his watermelon was taken, and it disappeared.

Now let's look at another example of how some big something can become taken from us without our knowing it. Here in 1 Kings 20:39, a man is lost. A grown man just disappears. And all that is known is that on the day of accountability, the man was not there. You remember this story. A king's servant has gone into battle, and a prisoner was brought to him with these instructions: You are to keep this prisoner at all costs, which includes your own life. He took the prisoner, and, at the beginning, we see he was in full military dress. He marched back and forth; 1, 2, 3, 4. 1, 2, 3, 4. Column right, march, 1, 2, 3, 4. There was no foolishness here. There was no way that the servant would be overcome by a stronger power. He was well-equipped, and he understood his responsibility and the seriousness of it. But when the king returned, the prisoner was gone. All that the servant could say was, "Master, as thy servant was busy here and there, the prisoner was gone." His watermelon, the size of a man, was gone.

Now I have no trouble believing that young man's watermelon story, do you? Oh, today I would say that more homes are lost and more church folk fall by the wayside during this time (busy here and there), and the watermelons were lost while they were busy here and there. And this might well be the cry of this age. While we've been busy here and there, someone's personal relationship with God has been stolen. Someone's sense of direction and their sense of belonging and the knowledge of who they are all were taken while the guardian was busy here and there. Now I am beginning to see how that watermelon was taken without the young man knowing it.

So with all of this gone, we are left without a dream or any sense of joyful enthusiasm for life. Therefore, that watermelon soon becomes a wearisome burden. (And let me say here that when our faith and our religion and our church become a burden, then any part of spiritual life can become lost, and we will never know that it is gone. When the joy and the excitement of it is gone, it can all be taken without our knowing it.) I heard a person say of a certain congregation near where we live, "They are the most joyless people I know." People get like this so easy. One night while I was a patient in the hospital, I couldn't sleep, and at 3:00 A.M. I was sitting on the side of the bed writing a sermon. A little nurse came in and wanted to know what I was doing. I said to her, "I am writing a sermon." She wanted to know what the sermon was about, and I told her that I was going to entitle it, "Are you sure you still have your watermelon?" And then I told her the story about the young man in the restaurant who had lost his watermelon. Then I went on to tell her that our watermelon can be something like (a) our quality of life (b) our divine knowledge of who we are (c) our direction of life or (d) our dream or our heavenly joy.

When I said "joy," she broke in and said, "Now I know what you mean, and I know a nurse here in this hospital. A few years ago, she was the most joyful person I have ever known. But then one day someone was promoted ahead of her, and since then she has not only lost her watermelon, but she don't even know where the patch is." You see, when someone has lost the joy to life and what they are doing in His kingdom, and then they lose that divine sense of it, then they forget the way home. And then, the thrill of worship, and the thrill of giving and being a part of all that God is doing, can just disappear. But you know, Jesus met people every day who had lost their watermelons. Some of those melons were humongous. Some of them made this man's melon look like a peanut. Now, I know you would expect me to say something about the prodigal and all that he lost. And in thinking of this story, I do want to be fair. But I must confess, so many preachers miss so much when relating what he lost in his watermelon. Oh yes, I admit that when the boy returned home he received a coat, a new pair of shoes, a ring, his bed, and his room, but he lost some things that could never be returned. Just think of all the days and the weeks and months he could have spent with his loving father, but that time was gone. Or just think of the innocence of all those young boys and girls he helped lead astray with his wild parties. He didn't have them by himself. Those watermelons of his were gone forever.

Now back to that young man in the restaurant, and, you know, more and more, I see that his watermelon could have just slipped out of his grasp, and he was not even aware of it. He was left holding nothing but empty space. You see, I think he began by losing his direction in life. Then he lost his best selfhood. Then he became careless in spiritual habits. This led to a time when he never thought of checking on himself, and then his watermelon was lost. Yes, I believe that this was where his watermelon got away from him.

The Bible lists several strong spiritual persons who lost their melons. Let's just call some of them to testify how they lost what they lost. For example, let's just call the man David. And we will say, "What happened to you, David? And he will reply, "Sir, I just forgot who I was and who that other man's wife was, and the evil voice became so loud that I couldn't hear my own inner voice. If I had just been employed spiritually, it would not have happened." Or we could call Judas and say, "Judas, can a person lose everything good and honorable and respectable over a thing like the quest for more power?" He'd answer, "Yes." "Yes," he would say, "I know that the whole thing can be lost."

But did you know that a nation can lose its watermelon? For example, look at Germany. Germany lost its watermelon. Did you know that at one time, Germany was the Christian center of the world? Germany was the seat of the Reformation. At the close of World War II, the World Wide Board of Evangelism met in Paris, France. There were eight or ten German religious leaders present who had escaped Hitler's gas chamber. You see, Hitler was intent on making life hell for Deitrick Boenhoffer, but these men managed to escape that awful death. These men sat at the table in France and told their stories of how Germany was lost.

The religious leaders said, "When Hitler took over, the Gestapo took over, they came first and got the sick, the lame, the unemployable, and they would meet with the church and tell us how important we were to Germany. Our job was to bury the dead and marry the young, but never to interfere with what the government was doing. Since we were not the sick, lame, or unemployed, we didn't say anything. We just did the burying and marrying. But then the army troops came and took the unionists because Hitler said that they were not good for the country. He kept saying to us, 'But you are valuable to Germany. You are needed to bury the dead and to marry the young, but you are not to object to what we are doing.' Since we were not unionist, we didn't say anything. We kept getting better and better and better at it. But then they came and got the Jews. Hitler told us that Germany didn't need all these foreigners, they were bad for the country. And again, he told us how important we were to the country, that we were to bury the dead and marry the young. But we were not to object to what the government did. So, we didn't object. But then when he came to get us, there was no one left to object. We had become masters at marrying the young and burying the dead, but we had lost the church." (The watermelon was gone.)

Dr. E. Stanley Jones, in relating this story at the Ashram at Wood College said that these men took their fists and hit on the pews where they sat and said, "We became masters at doing unimportant things, and oh, we lost our church and nation."

So what this story says to us is when we lose our sense of direction, we are in danger of losing our sense of belonging. And if we lose our sense of belonging, we will soon lose our best self. If we lose our best self, the watermelon is gone.

Now what advice do I have to the man who lost his watermelon? You go and find the Lord of the patch. He has a watermelon just for you. One that meets your needs. You will find that He is the Good Shepherd who left the ninety-nine in search of one. You will probably find that this Lord of the patch was right behind you when you lost your watermelon and was ready to restore it. Yes, He owns the patch and wants you to have your melon just as it was before. What a great friend this Lord of the patch is to all of us. Amen.

Is your watermelon secure?

About the Author

*H*uey Wood was born in 1921 in Union County, Mississippi. He had ten brothers and sisters, including his twin brother, Hulet. Huey joined the army in 1939 and rose to the level of master sergeant. During World War II, he took part in the invasion of Morocco and later guarded President Roosevelt at Casablanca during his conference with Winston Churchill. He was awarded a Purple Heart and a Bronze Star.

After the war, Huey met Ruth Mayhew, who had just graduated from Wood Junior College. They were married one month later. In 1958 the Woods moved to Etta, Mississippi, where they both received the call to preach. Huey was officially assigned two charges in the Booneville, Mississippi area, one with five churches and one with three. His wife was the first woman ordained in the Methodist Church in Mississippi. They served over the years at Belmont, Corinth, Southaven, Olive Branch, and Byhalia, Mississippi. In 1988, the Woods officially retired from the ministry.

Since 1988, Huey has served the Robinsonville United Methodist Church in Robinsonville, Mississippi. Huey and Ruth currently reside in Olive Branch, Mississippi. They have two sons, eight grandchildren, and eight great-grandchildren.